SPACE SHUTTLE

PICTURE LIBRARY
SPACE SHUTTLE

N. S. Barrett

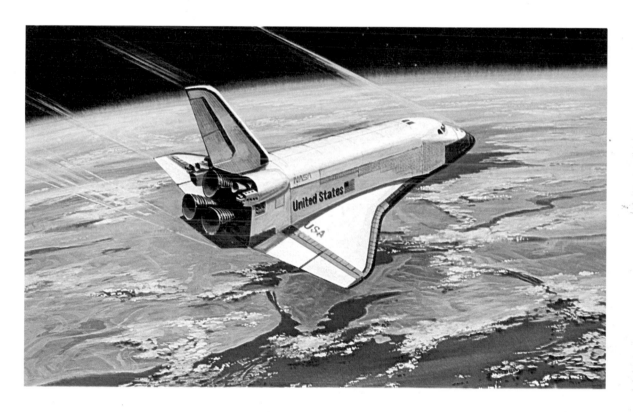

Franklin Watts

London   New York   Sydney   Toronto

© 1985 Franklin Watts Ltd

First published in Great Britain
   1985 by
Franklin Watts Ltd
12a Golden Square
London W1

First published in the USA by
Franklin Watts Inc
387 Park Avenue South
New York
N.Y. 10016

First published in Australia by
Franklin Watts
1 Campbell Street
Artarmon, NSW 2064

UK ISBN: 0 86313 224 3
US ISBN: 0-531-04949-3
Library of Congress Catalog
 Card Number 84-52003

Printed in Italy

Designed by
Barrett & Willard

Illustrations
The photographs and
drawings are reproduced
by kind permission of
the National Aeronautics
and Space Administration
(NASA) of the United States

Technical Consultant
Robin Kerrod

Contents

Introduction

The Space Shuttle takes people up into space and brings them back again. It lifts off like a rocket, and travels in space like a spacecraft. Then it returns to Earth and lands like an airplane.

   The main part of the Shuttle is the orbiter. It goes up with two rockets and a large fuel tank. These are pushed away when used up.

△ An orbiter circles the Earth. The Moon can be seen in the distance. The position and direction of the craft may be changed by firing small rockets, called thrusters.

An important use of the Space Shuttle is to take satellites into space. The orbiter has a large cargo bay for carrying them. A Shuttle's cargo is also called its payload.

A crew of up to seven people can be carried in the orbiter. You do not have to be a fully trained astronaut to travel in the Space Shuttle.

△ Astronaut Gordon Fullerton begins to prepare a meal. Every piece of equipment is attached to the walls of the cabin. Otherwise it would float all over the place.

The Space Shuttle

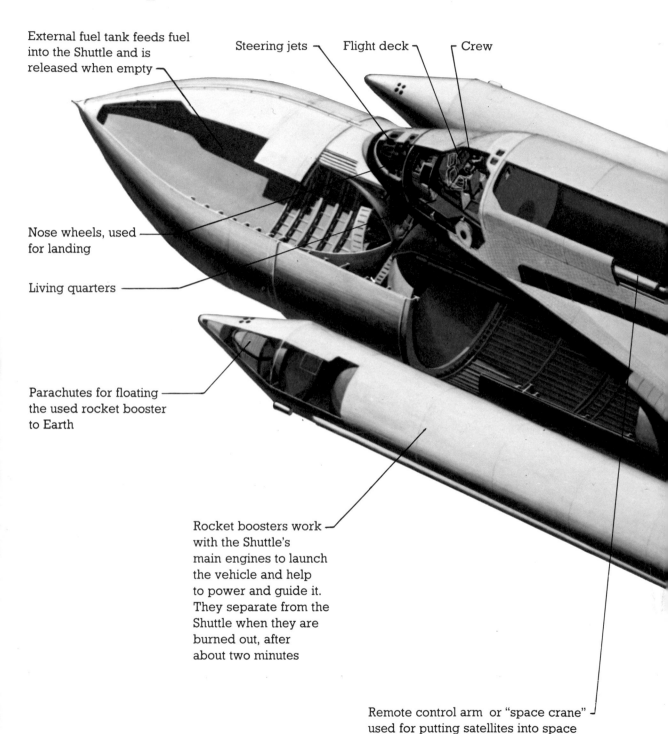

External fuel tank feeds fuel into the Shuttle and is released when empty

Steering jets

Flight deck

Crew

Nose wheels, used for landing

Living quarters

Parachutes for floating the used rocket booster to Earth

Rocket boosters work with the Shuttle's main engines to launch the vehicle and help to power and guide it. They separate from the Shuttle when they are burned out, after about two minutes

Remote control arm or "space crane" used for putting satellites into space

8

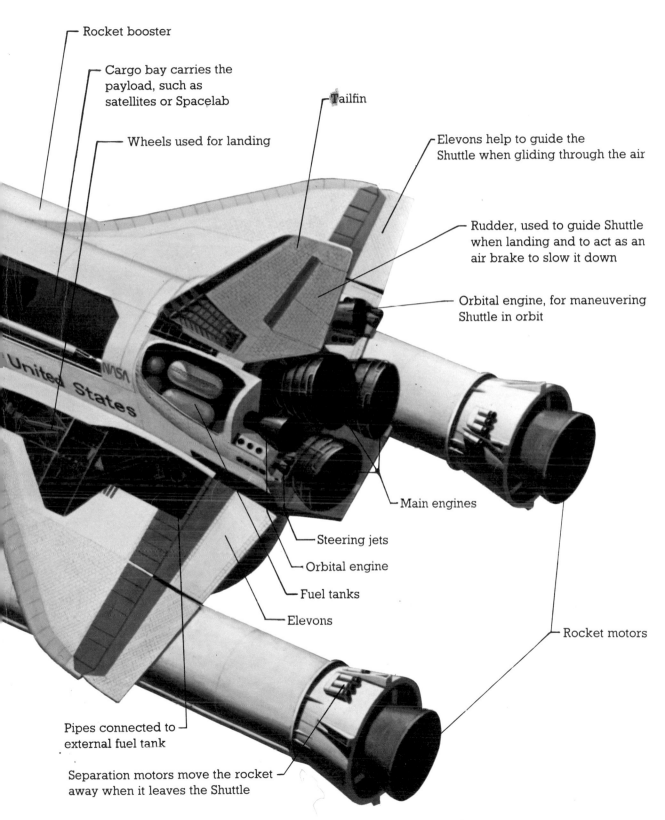

Rocket booster

Cargo bay carries the payload, such as satellites or Spacelab

Tailfin

Wheels used for landing

Elevons help to guide the Shuttle when gliding through the air

Rudder, used to guide Shuttle when landing and to act as an air brake to slow it down

Orbital engine, for maneuvering Shuttle in orbit

United States

NASA

Main engines

Steering jets

Orbital engine

Fuel tanks

Elevons

Rocket motors

Pipes connected to external fuel tank

Separation motors move the rocket away when it leaves the Shuttle

9

The launch

Most Shuttle launches are made from the Kennedy Space Center at Cape Canaveral, Florida. The Shuttle fleet has four orbiters – *Columbia, Challenger, Discovery* and *Atlantis.*

An orbiter is designed to last for at least 100 flights. The rockets may be reused about 20 times.

△ The Space Shuttle is carried slowly to the launch pad by a crawler-transporter. This is called the roll-out.

The Shuttle is prepared for launch in the Vehicle Assembly Building. The two rockets are built up on a mobile platform and the external fuel tank is attached. Then the orbiter with its payload on board is fixed to the tank. A giant transporter takes the Shuttle and platform to the launch pad.

▽ Astronauts Ken Mattingly and Henry Hartsfield have their equipment checked ready for the launch.

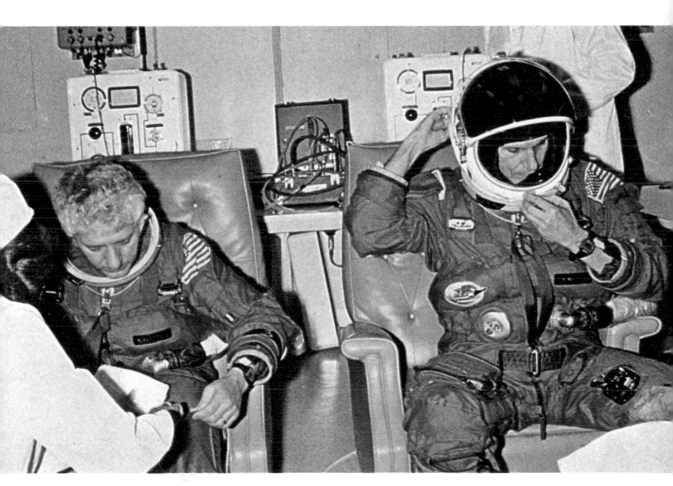

The crew enters the Shuttle on the launch pad. The countdown to liftoff begins. All the systems are checked. If there is something wrong, the launch might have to be put back to a later date.

The orbiter's main engines ignite first and build up to full power. Then the huge solid rockets ignite and the Shuttle lifts off.

▷ **With rockets burning and engines firing, the Space Shuttle lifts off.**

▽ **The Shuttle stands on the launch pad, ready for liftoff.**

Boosters away

The solid rockets burn out after about two minutes. They are separated from the tank and float down to the ocean on parachutes. Special recovery ships tow the rocket casings to land.

It takes the Shuttle about eight minutes to reach the edge of space. The empty external tank is then detached from the orbiter.

▽ The solid rocket boosters are cast off from the Shuttle when their fuel is used up.

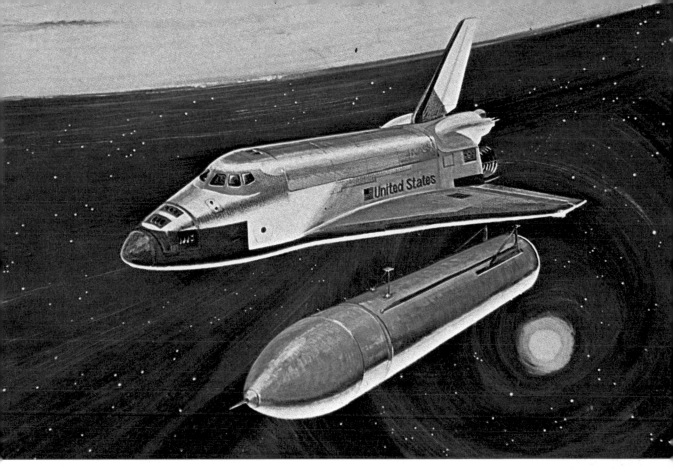

△ The empty fuel tank is released from the orbiter. It breaks up over the ocean when it returns to the Earth's atmosphere.

◁ The empty rocket cases are recovered at sea and may be used again.

Inside the Shuttle

Most Shuttle missions last for up to 10 days. The living quarters are more comfortable than those of the earlier manned spacecraft.

The cabin has two levels, a flight deck and a mid-deck. Astronauts operate the orbiter and control the manipulator arm from the flight deck. The crew members sleep and eat in the mid-deck area.

△ The forward flight deck of the orbiter.

▷ Astronaut Robert Crippen enjoys the sensation of weightlessness in the mid-deck section of the orbiter.

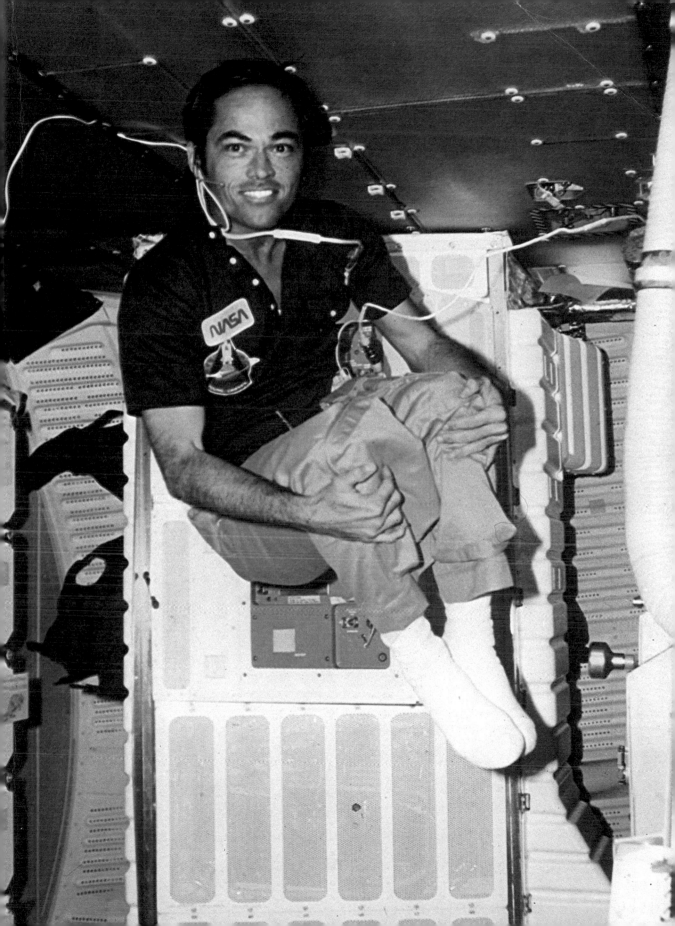

The mission commander and another pilot operate the flight controls. At the back of the flight deck, another astronaut looks out over the cargo bay and operates the manipulator arm.

Payload controls are also located on the flight deck. These may be operated by payload specialists, who do not need to be full-time astronauts.

△ In space if you want to read it, you have to catch it first, as astronaut Richard Truly finds out.

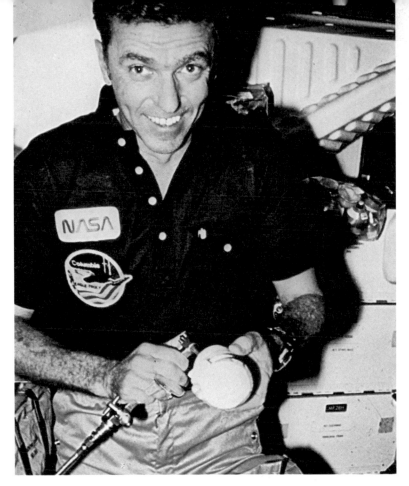

◁ Astronaut Engle
prepares a drink.
Drinks are made from
dried powder. Water is
inserted into the drink
container through a
hollow needle. Straws
are used for drinking.

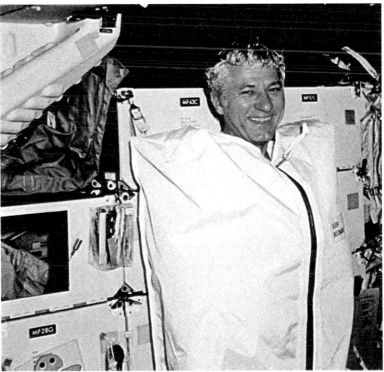

◁ Astronaut Hartsfield
is strapped into his
sleeping bag ready for
bed. In space, it does
not matter whether you
sleep lying down or
standing up, so long as
you are strapped in to
keep from floating
about the cabin.

The orbiter crew members have a busy working day. As well as putting satellites and other spacecraft into space, they carry out tests on themselves and on animals and plants. They keep a careful check on the effects of living in orbit, where there is no effective gravity.

The crew also gather important information about the Earth from special cameras on the orbiter.

△ Astronaut Jack Lousma with an experiment on board *Columbia*. He is studying the effects of space travel on insects.

▷ Astronaut Joe Allen takes part in a medical test.

Payloads

The cargo bay takes up half the length of the orbiter. It is big enough to hold several satellites.

It can carry a complete scientific laboratory called Spacelab. Up to four people, who eat and sleep in the orbiter, carry out tests inside Spacelab and use instruments mounted outside it.

▽ Satellites and packages of different shapes and sizes are packed into the cargo bay.

◁ Astronaut Story Musgrave works in the open cargo bay. Special space suits must be worn for work outside the orbiter.

▽ A drawing of Spacelab in the cargo bay is cut away to show the people working inside it.

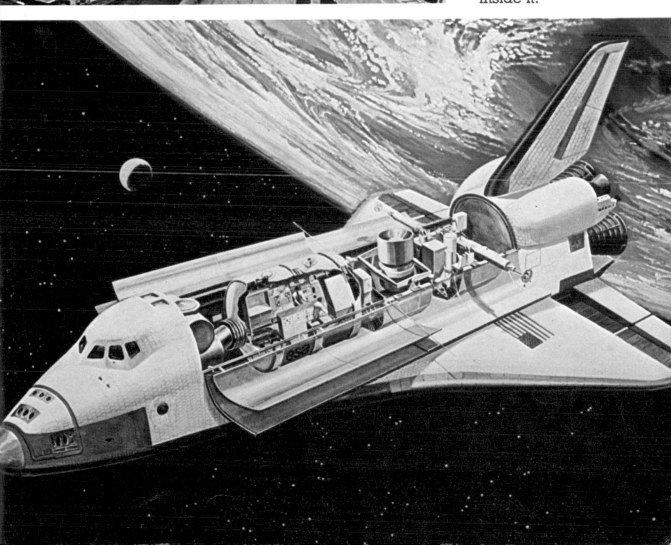

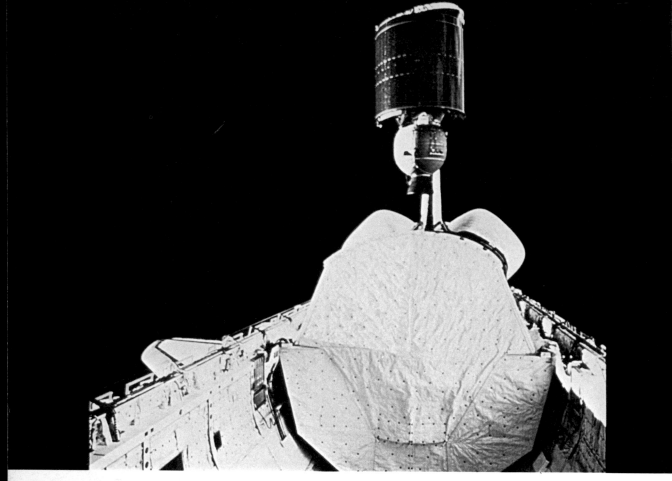

△ A satellite is
released from the
cargo bay of the
orbiter.

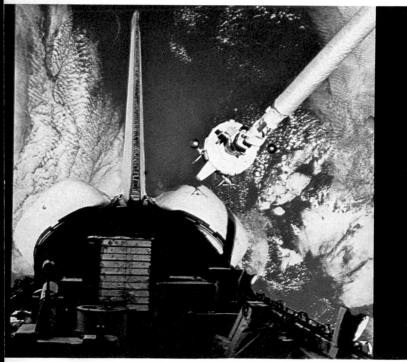

◁ The manipulator arm
is used to lift a package
containing an
experiment.

Re-entry

Re-entry is when the orbiter returns to the Earth's atmosphere. At this stage it is traveling very fast.

The crew puts on special pressure suits for returning to the Earth's gravity. These stop the blood draining to the lower part of the body and causing blackouts. The crew also puts on helmets.

▽ During re-entry, contact with the air causes great heat. The outside of the orbiter is protected by special tiles. These become red hot on the outside, but the heat does not go through them.

Landing

Two hours before landing, the orbiter crew strap themselves into their seats. The pilot uses small engines to make the craft fall out of its orbit.

The pilot lines the craft up with the landing strip and it glides down without engines. The landing wheels come down as it levels off and it touches down like an airplane.

▽ Two escort planes accompany *Columbia* as it glides down toward the landing strip.

△ The orbiter's rear wheels touch down during a perfect landing.

◁ The crew of *Challenger* at the landing ceremony after its first mission in 1983.

The story of the Shuttle

Before the Shuttle

The exploration of space began in 1957 when the Russians launched Sputnik I. This was the first spacecraft to orbit the Earth. Soon both the Russians and the Americans were sending men into space. In 1969 American astronauts landed on the Moon. Unmanned spacecraft were sent to explore the planets and some went even farther into space. All of these projects cost enormous amounts of money.

The huge rockets used to launch

△ A jumbo jet carries *Enterprise* up for a test flight.

Back and forth

In the 1970s, the United States decided to build a spacecraft that could be used again and again. The term "shuttle" comes from weaving. It is the part of the loom that moves back and forth. This is what Space Shuttle does.

The National Aeronautics and Space Administration (NASA) needed a low-cost method for continuing the space program.

△ Testing an early orbiter model.

the spacecraft fell away when they had done their job. Only a small part of the spacecraft returned to Earth with the astronauts. On the first manned Moon mission, for example, the Command Module that returned to Earth was only a thirtieth the size of the vehicle launched.

△ *Enterprise* is released from the plane and begins its first flight.

There were several designs and much research was done before the final choice was made.

△ The launching of the first Space Shuttle. *Columbia* lifts off.

Piggyback

A special Shuttle orbiter was built for tests. This trial, or prototype, orbiter was called *Enterprise*, named for the spaceship in the TV series *Star Trek*. It did not have working engines or a heat shield. The idea was to test how well it would glide through the Earth's atmosphere and land.

For these trials, the *Enterprise* was taken up on top of a modified Boeing 747 airliner, riding "piggyback." It was first released from the jumbo jet in August 1977. Two astronauts piloted it to Earth from a height of 4.3 miles (7 km). They landed it safely on a dry lake in the Mojave Desert, in California.

First flight

The first orbiter to fly in space was *Columbia*. It was launched from Cape Canaveral on April 12, 1981, with astronauts John Young and Robert Crippen aboard. It was successfully maneuvered into orbit and various tests were carried out over two days. Then on April 14 it was brought down to a perfect landing at Edwards Airforce Base, in California.

△ Astronauts Musgrave and Peterson make the first orbiter space walk.

Growth of the fleet

The second orbiter, *Challenger*, made its maiden voyage in April 1983. During this mission the astronauts made the first space walk from an orbiter.

With each Shuttle flight, more astronauts and scientists gain experience of space travel. More satellites are placed into orbit and more knowledge is brought back to Earth.

Facts and records

△ Bruce McCandless uses a jet-powered backpack to move through space alone.

Walking alone

Astronaut Bruce McCandless was the first person to venture into space without being tied to a spacecraft. He made his historic space walk from the orbiter *Challenger* in February 1984.

First women

With the Space Shuttle women began to play a bigger part in the space program. In 1983 Sally Ride became the first American woman to venture into space. In

1984 Kathryn Sullivan was the first American woman to walk in space.

△ Sally Ride.

Getaway specials

On each Shuttle mission there is usually some spare space for extra payload. For just a few thousand dollars an organization, a college or a private person can book a "getaway special." This is a small container that will carry an experiment on the Shuttle.

△ Getaway specials may be mounted on the sides of the cargo bay.

Glossary

External tank
The large fuel tank outside the orbiter that feeds fuel in and is released when empty.

Heat shield
The special tiles on the outside of the orbiter that protect it and the crew from the heat of re-entry.

Ignite
When engines start up they ignite.

Liftoff
The moment when the Shuttle rises off the launch pad.

Mission specialist
A fully trained astronaut who is in charge of the payload and other scientific experiments on the mission.

Orbit
The path a satellite takes around a larger body. The Earth is in orbit around the Sun. The Shuttle orbiter is launched into orbit around the Earth.

Orbiter
The spacecraft part of the Shuttle. There are four orbiters in the Shuttle fleet.

Payload
Everything taken up in the orbiter as part of an experiment or which will be placed in orbit.

Re-entry
The point of return to the Earth's atmosphere.

Solid rocket boosters
The two rockets powered by solid fuel that provide most of the thrust at liftoff. They are recovered and used again.

Space Shuttle
The complete vehicle that lifts off, consisting of the orbiter, the two solid rocket boosters and the external fuel tank.

Space walk
A space walk is any astronaut activity outside a spacecraft. It is also called extravehicular activity, or EVA.

Weightlessness
When a spacecraft travels around the Earth in orbit, things and people can float around inside it. This state is called weightlessness. The proper name for it is "free fall" because everyone and everything are falling together around the Earth.

Index